CW00400692

70000 0000 32547

BRIGHT IDEA BOOKS

Lakes IN THE Ocean: COOL UNDERWATER FACTS

by Kimberly M. Hutmacher

raintree

a Capstone company — publishers for children

Raintree is an imprint of Capstone Global Library Limited, a company incorporated in England and Wales having its registered office at 264 Banbury Road, Oxford, OX2 7DY – Registered company number: 6695582

www.raintree.co.uk
myorders@raintree.co.uk

Edited by Meg Gaertner
Designed by Becky Daum
Production by Colleen McLaren
Printed and bound in India

ISBN 978 1 4747 7457 4 (hardback)
ISBN 978 1 4747 8242 5 (paperback)

British Library Cataloguing in Publication Data
A full catalogue record for this book is available from the British Library.

Acknowledgements
We would like to thank the following for permission to reproduce photographs: iStockphoto: baona, 5, beusbeus, 21, Eric Broder Van Dyke, 23, rightdx, 25, 28, RyanJLane, 24–25; NASA: JPL, 7; NOAA: Gavin Eppard, WHOI/Expedition to the Deep Slope/OER, 14–15, IFE, URI–IAO, UW, Lost City Science Party/OAR/OER/The Lost City 2005 Expedition, 13, NSF, 17, Pacific Ring of Fire 2004 Expedition/NOAA Office of Ocean Exploration/Dr. Bob Embley, NOAA PMEL, Chief Scientist, 18–19, Rhode Island Institute for Archaeological Oceanography/Secrets of the Gulf Expedition/NOS/NMS/FGBNMS, 8–9; Shutterstock Images: Alexeysun, 30–31, Ethan Daniels, 27, Khoroshunova Olga, 10, Neil Bromhall, 26, SNT4, cover, Vadim Petrakov, 11
Every effort has been made to contact copyright holders of material reproduced in this book. Any omissions will be rectified in subsequent printings if notice is given to the publisher.

We would like to thank Hans G. Dam, PhD, Professor of Marine Science, for his help with this book.

CONTENTS

AMAZING Underwater World

There are forests in the ocean. There are lakes and waterfalls too. Some ocean fish light up. Others have no faces. The ocean is amazing!

Many deep-sea creatures give off their own light.

WILD
Water

Ocean covers 71 per cent of Earth. It has an average depth of 3,780 metres (12,400 feet). Visible light cannot pass below 100 metres (330 feet). The ocean is pitch black below that level.

Images from space show how much of Earth is covered by water.

An underwater lake formed
in the Gulf of Mexico,
off the coast of Texas, USA.

LAKES IN THE OCEAN

Rock and salt form the ocean floor. There is water beneath the floor. Sometimes the water seeps up through the salt. It **dissolves** the salt. The ocean floor sinks. The salt water fills the space left behind. This water is saltier than ocean water. It is very **dense**. It does not mix with the ocean water. Instead, it forms an underwater lake.

UNDERWATER WATERFALL

Some waterfalls are underwater. One is in the Denmark Strait. This is between Greenland and Iceland. Cold water is denser than hot water. Cold water sinks. It drops straight down. It forms an underwater ocean waterfall. The water drops about 3,500 metres (11,500 feet).

There is an underwater waterfall off the coast of Mauritius, an island nation east of Africa.

Angel Falls is in Venezuela.

RECORD HEIGHTS

The tallest land waterfall is Angel Falls. It is 979 m (3,211 feet) tall. But the Denmark Strait waterfall is three times taller.

CHAPTER 3

IN THE
Depths

The largest mountain range is the Mid-ocean Ridge. It is 65,000 kilometres (40,400 miles) long. It is underwater. Some of its peaks rise above sea level. It covers almost a quarter of Earth's surface.

A jellyfish swims next to a formation in the Mid-Atlantic Ridge, part of the Mid-ocean Ridge.

CHALLENGER DEEP

The Mariana Trench is in the Pacific Ocean. It is a canyon. The ocean's deepest point is there. This point is called Challenger Deep. It is about 10,990 metres (36,070 feet) deep. The **water pressure** is very heavy. It is 1,000 times greater than at sea level. Imagine 50 jumbo jets on top of you. That is what Challenger Deep would feel like.

The *Alvin* has taken three people to an ocean depth of 7,000 m (23,200 feet).

CHAPTER 4

UNDERWATER
Fires

The Earth's surface is divided into pieces. They are called **tectonic plates**. Sometimes their movements create volcanoes. Most volcanic eruptions happen in the ocean. They happen underwater. **Lava** flows along the ocean floor.

BIRTH OF AN ISLAND

An ocean volcano erupts. The lava cools. It hardens. More layers form over time. The volcano gets bigger. It reaches the ocean's surface. Then it forms an island.

Lava spews as an underwater volcano erupts.

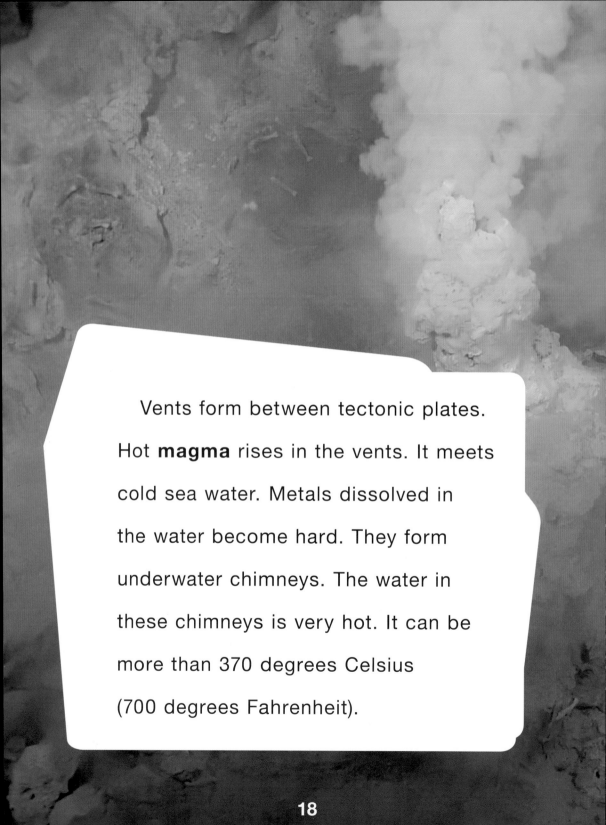

Vents form between tectonic plates. Hot **magma** rises in the vents. It meets cold sea water. Metals dissolved in the water become hard. They form underwater chimneys. The water in these chimneys is very hot. It can be more than 370 degrees Celsius (700 degrees Fahrenheit).

The water in the chimneys can get twice as hot as the temperature needed to cook a chicken.

CHAPTER 5

OCEAN
Plants

Oceans have forests. Giant kelp is the largest form of seaweed. It grows in underwater forests. It can grow more than 30 metres (100 feet) tall. Oceans also have grass. Seagrasses are underwater plants. Their beds can grow large. Some can even be seen from space!

Schools of fish swim through kelp forests.

ONLY SO DEEP

Plants need sunlight to survive. Ocean plants don't grow in the deepest parts. They live in the top 100 metres (330 feet) of the water. There is not enough sunlight below that depth.

CHAPTER 6

OCEAN
Animals

Scientists know of more than 200,000 ocean **species**. But they believe there are millions more. More than 80 per cent of the ocean is still unexplored.

The blue whale is the largest animal ever. Its heart is the size of a car. Oarfish are the longest fish. They have snakelike bodies. They can grow to be 17 metres (56 feet) long!

Oarfish usually live in the deep sea. Dead ones sometimes wash up on the shore.

An octopus is an amazing animal. It can change colour. It can shoot out ink to protect itself. An octopus can squeeze through tiny holes. It can solve problems. It can use tools. Scientists think it can even learn from experience.

Octopus arms are covered in suckers that can grasp objects.

There are more than
300 species of squid
in the world.

The giant squid can grow

to be 10 metres (33 feet) long.

It has the largest eyes of all

animals. Each eye is about the

size of a dinner plate.

Anglerfish wait until their prey is in range. Then they attack.

DEEP-SEA CREATURES

Some fish have clear skin. Some glow in the dark. An anglerfish has a built-in fishing pole. A growth on its head gives off light. The light attracts prey.

The frilled shark is a **living fossil**. It has not changed much in millions of years. It looks like a thick eel. A real deep-sea eel has no face. Its mouth pops out to catch food. Then its mouth goes back inside its body.

The hairy frogfish is another ocean creature. Instead of swimming, it walks on its fins.

GLOSSARY

dense
closely compacted and thick

dissolve
When a solid is mixed into
and becomes part of a liquid

lava
molten rock that forms from
magma that has been cooled

living fossil
an animal that closely looks
or seems like an ancient
creature

magma
hot fluid underneath the
Earth's surface

species
a group of plants or animals
of the same kind that can
produce offspring together

tectonic plate
a large piece of the Earth's
top layer that can move along
the Earth's surface

water pressure
the force of the water pushing
down on a certain area

1. Ocean animals make plenty of noise. But there are other ocean sounds that scientists cannot explain. They could be from icebergs breaking apart. They could be from unknown animals.

2. Coral is a tiny creature. Corals make a sort of skeleton out of their bodies. These skeletons pile up over time. They form massive coral reefs. Coral also makes its own sunscreen to protect itself from the Sun. Scientists are studying coral to create better sunscreen for people.

3. There are more artefacts on the ocean floor than in all museums combined. These include items from about one million shipwrecks.

ACTIVITY

SALT WATER VS. FRESH WATER

Almost all of Earth's water, including the water in the oceans, is salt water. Learn what happens when salt is added to water through this experiment.

You will need:

1 bunch of grapes

3 tall glasses of water

2 tablespoons of salt

2 tablespoons of sugar

2 tablespoons of cornflour

1 spoon for stirring

1. Mix the salt into one glass of water. Stir until you can no longer see the salt. Label this glass "salt".

2. Repeat step one for the sugar and the cornflour. Use the other two glasses of water.

3. Drop a few grapes into each glass. Do the grapes float or sink?

Salt water is denser than fresh water. It sinks underneath objects that are less dense. Many objects that sink in fresh water will float in salt water.

FIND OUT MORE

Ready to dive into more amazing ocean facts? Check out these resources.

Books

Deep Oceans (Earth's Last Frontiers), Ellen Labrecque (Raintree, 2015)

Oceans (Fascinating Facts) (Collins, 2016)

Ultimate Oceanpedia: The Most Complete Ocean Reference Ever, Christina Wilsdon (National Geographic Kids, 2016)

Websites

National Geographic Kids: Ocean
www.natgeokids.com/uk/discover/geography/general-geography/ocean-facts

WWF: Oceans Fact Files
gowild.wwf.org.uk/regions/oceans-fact-files

DK Find Out!: Deep-Sea Fish
www.dkfindout.com/uk/animals-and-nature/fish/deep-sea-fish/octopuses/

INDEX